DIVING
BASICS
by **Bob Goldberg**

Illustrations by
Art Seiden

With Photographs

Created and Produced by
Arvid Knudsen

PRENTICE-HALL, Inc.
Englewood Cliffs, New Jersey

ACKNOWLEDGEMENTS: SPECIAL THANKS ARE DUE MIKE CECATIELLO, PAM HESTER, DALE DMITRZAK, COLETTE BIZAL, BECKY BINNEY, JIM EBERT, CATHY WENTZ, PAT McFADDEN, MAUREEN BRECKINRIDGE, PATTI JONES, AND MARY ELLEN CLARK FOR PARTICIPATING IN THE DIVING PHOTOGRAPHS FOR THIS BOOK.

PHOTOGRAPHS IN THIS BOOK ARE COURTESY OF BOB GOLDBERG WITH AN ASSIST BY TIM JONES.

Other **Sports Basics Books** in Series

BASKETBALL BASICS *by Greggory Morris*

RUNNING BASICS *by Carol Lea Benjamin*

DISCO BASICS *by Maxine Polley*

GYMNASTICS BASICS *by John and Mary Jean Traetta*

RACQUETBALL BASICS *by Tony Boccaccio*

FRISBEE DISC BASICS *by Dan Roddick*

SWIMMING BASICS *by Rob Orr and Jane B. Tyler*

HORSEBACK RIDING BASICS *by Dianne Reimer*

SKIING BASICS *by Al Morrozzi*

BASEBALL BASICS *by Jack Lang*

FISHING BASICS *by John Randolph*

FOOTBALL BASICS *by Larry Fox*

SOCCER BASICS *by Alex Yannis*

SAILING BASICS *by Lorna Slocombe*

BICYCLING BASICS *by Tim and Glenda Wilhelm*

BACKPACKING BASICS *by John Randolph*

TENNIS BASICS *by Robert J. LaMarche*

TRACK & FIELD BASICS *by Fred McMane*

HOCKEY BASICS *by Norman MacLean*

BOWLING BASICS *by Chuck Pezzano*

KARATE BASICS *by Thomas J. Nardi*

ICE-SKATING BASICS *by Norman MacLean*

WATERSPORTS BASICS *by Don Wallace*

CAMPING BASICS *by Wayne Armstrong*

BOATING BASICS *by Henry F. Halsted*

GOLF BASICS *by Roger Schiffman*

WRESTLING BASICS *by Ron Fox*

Printed in the United States of America   · J

Prentice-Hall International (UK) Limited, London
Prentice-Hall of Australia, Pty. Ltd., Sydney
Prentice-Hall of Canada, Inc., Toronto
Prentice-Hall Hispanoamericana, S.A., Mexico
Prentice-Hall of India Private Ltd., New Delhi
Prentice-Hall of Japan, Inc., Tokyo
Prentice-Hall of Southeast Asia Pte. Ltd., Singapore
Whitehall Books Limited, Wellington, New Zealand
Editora Prentice-Hall do Brasil Ltda., Rio de Janeiro

10 9 8 7 6 5 4 3 2 1

Library of Congress Cataloging in Publication Data

Goldberg, Bob, 1946–
    Diving basics.

    Summary: Presents a brief history of diving and describes diving techniques, emphasizing requirements for competition.
    1. Diving—Juvenile literature. [1. Diving]
I. Seiden, Art, ill. II. Knudsen, Arvid. III. Title.
GV837.6.G65   1986   797.2   85-25773
ISBN 0-13-215963-5

CONTENTS

An Introduction
to Competitive Diving / 1

Diving, in its purest form, is both the expression of art and the epitome of sport. There is only you, the springboard, and the pool. Whether you are attempting a forward dive from the one-meter board or a back three-and-one-half somersault from the ten-meter platform, you are creating an artistic movement that all can admire and competing in a tremendous sporting event at the same time.

Competitive diving as an organized sport has only a brief history of about 100 years. Way back around 480 B.C., the first etching of a figure diving was found on a burial vault in South Naples, Italy, named the Toumbe del Tuffatore (the Tomb of the Diver). But there is no recorded history of diving as a sport until the early nineteenth century, when the Greeks and the Swedes performed gymnastic stunts from apparatus positioned over water.

In 1883, the Amateur Swimming Association of England began a "plunging" competition. (It was really a plunge-and-glide competition for distance.) In 1889, Scotland held its first diving championships. And in 1895, the Royal Lifesaving Society of Great Britain held its first National Graceful Diving Championships.

5

A Front Hurdle.

At the International Olympics of 1904 in St. Louis, Missouri—the site of the first Olympic diving events—the United States team won several gold medals. In 1907, the University of Pennsylvania began what was to become the oldest diving meet in the United States. In 1912, women entered the Olympic diving competitions. In that same year, Stanford University, in California, hired the first full-time diving coach, Ernest Brandsten, a Swedish Olympian.

The NCAA (National Collegiate Athletic Association) organized the sport of diving for colleges in 1924. Private clubs, Y's, high schools, and other organizations followed through with diving programs for youngsters over the years. By now, almost 100 years of dedication on the parts of coaches, young athletes, and parents have gone into the development of the sport and art of diving.

The difficulties encountered, the many challenges to mind and body, the excitement of the diving meet and competition, the people, and the artistic expression of the athletes are what the sport is all about. To get you started, you will need a qualified coach, proper pool facilities, and a good well-balanced training program. It takes years of hard work and commitment to become an exceptional diver. It has been said that once you dive into this sport, you may never want to get out.

So, welcome to the world of diving. If you are an aspiring young diver who is 8 to 14 years old, this book is for you. Begin by looking at the requirements to get started in this sport.

1. A Place to Practice You'll need to find a swimming pool that has the right equipment: A one-meter diving board is a must (39 inches above the water). It will help too if you have access to a three-meter board and a five-meter platform.

2. A Diving Club There are many organizations that sponsor diving. U.S. Diving is currently the largest national organizing body sponsoring national championships in several age groups. But you'll be able to find terrific programs in the Y's, Boys' and Girls' Clubs, and summer club programs. Perhaps even your school offers a competitive diving/swimming team.

A One-Half Twist Layout.

3. A Coach   You'll need someone who is interested in both you and the sport. Former divers are a great help, but many great coaches were never great divers. Most importantly, look for someone who cares!

4. You, the Diver   You'll need to learn the skills of the sport. To do this effectively, you should have enough swimming skills to be safe in the water. It will be helpful if you have a kinesthetic sense (an ability to feel where you are in space). Some people call this "natural talent."

Forward or Inward Dive Layout.

You and Your Body / 2

To develop into a top-notch diver, you need to become a finely tuned athlete in every sense of the word. Although recreational diving requires only a pool and a diving board to have some fun, competitive diving requires full-time dedication on your part and on the parts of your coach and your parents. Flexibility, general exercises, and body conditioning are important ingredients of a total program.

Following are some of the basic exercises you can do. This is not a complete program for everyone but only some pointers to get you started. With these, add new ideas and develop your own special program.

For Strength

1. Situps Your abdominal muscles require constant attention. Work on these situps until you can do 100 per day in 4 sets of 25 each. Try to keep your knees bent, feet under a bar, and hands behind your head.

2. Pushups These help you with general body toning and general body shape. Keep your back flat while practicing your pushups.

Try a variation with your toes pointed. Work so that you can do 25 pushups each day without stopping.

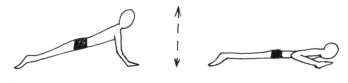

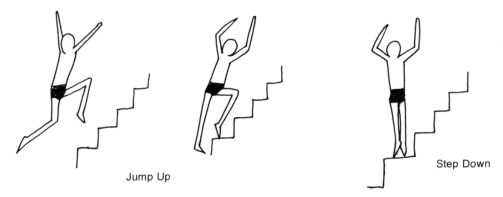

Jump Up

Step Down

3. Hurdle-Ups Dry-land hurdles add strength to your legs and are helpful in working on the form of your springboard hurdle. Do your dry-land hurdles by jumping from one leg, going up about two steps, and landing on both feet. Work at it so that you can hold your arms up as you land and keep your balance throughout.

Try to point your toes as you drive your knee up and jump.

Weight Training and Weight Lifting

There are many ideas and philosophies for training with weights. Each coach has his or her own opinion. But all agree that it is a mistake to start training with weights at too early an age. Wait until you're 15 years old before you check with your coach about starting a general strength development program. The goal of any weight-training program in your late teen years is to make you a stronger and better diver.

Endurance Conditioning

Diving by its very nature is an explosive sport that takes only two seconds to complete. It does not require a great deal of endurance to do one dive. But in order to complete a two-hour workout, a diving athlete needs endurance and stamina conditioning. Running, jogging, or swimming in addition to your diving practice will help you develop that stamina.

Diet

There is no one diet that all divers need to follow to be in proper condition for training and competition. A normal diet that consists of well-balanced meals in proper amounts is all that is necessary. In your later teen years, you may find that you need to monitor your body weight in order to look fit and trim while diving.

Flexibility

Making your body as flexible as possible is one of the most important aspects of your body conditioning. Good divers combine strength and explosiveness with body flexibility. Give attention to each part of your body as you spend at least 10 minutes each in stretching exercises before your full workout.

1. Shoulders The following three shoulder stretches can be helpful. Work into each one gradually.

Gradual lift   Lean against the wall   Gradual lift

2. Lower Back and Back of Legs Sit in an L position and lean forward until you feel the back of your legs just begin to hurt. Work on your stretch at this point. Be sure not to bounce in order to get down a little farther. Simply pull down a little bit at a time.

Try this variation in a straddle L position. Go to the left, center, then to the right. These exercises are similar to some of the drills in Chapter 4.

3. Toe Stretch A most important exercise! Kneel down and point your toes so that your weight rests on the front of your ankles and arms. Lift your knees from the ground as high as you can and slowly rock backward. As you get stronger and more flexible, you may be able to stand on your toes!

THE DIVING SPRINGBOARDS AND PLATFORMS

THIS SIMULATED DIAGRAM IS NOT MEANT TO SHOW WHAT OFFICIAL DIVING FACILITIES LOOK LIKE — BUT ONLY TO PROVIDE VISUAL INSIGHT. THE NCAA MINIMUM DIVING FACILITY DIMENSIONS, ADOPTED IN 1969, ARE THE RULE.

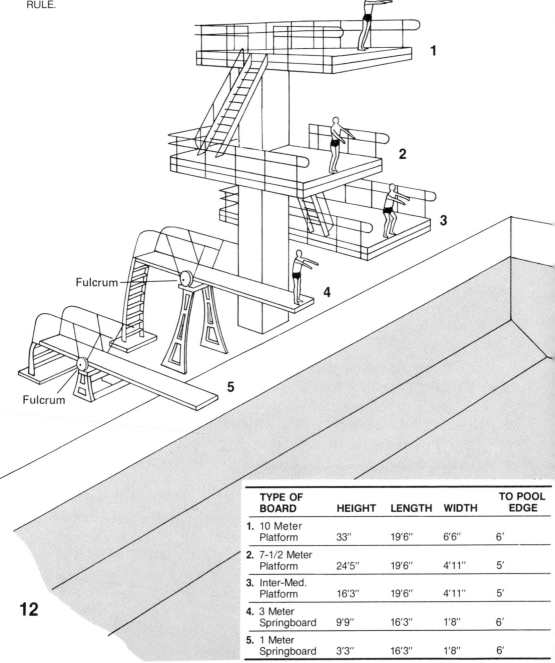

Fulcrum

Fulcrum

12

TYPE OF BOARD	HEIGHT	LENGTH	WIDTH	TO POOL EDGE
1. 10 Meter Platform	33″	19′6″	6′6″	6′
2. 7-1/2 Meter Platform	24′5″	19′6″	4′11″	5′
3. Inter-Med. Platform	16′3″	19′6″	4′11″	5′
4. 3 Meter Springboard	9′9″	16′3″	1′8″	6′
5. 1 Meter Springboard	3′3″	16′3″	1′8″	6′

Fundamentals of
Board Work / 3

Much of what happens to your dive once you are in the air and through to your entry into the water is determined during the front hurdle or the back press. This part of your dive is referred to as your board work. It is probably the single most important yet one of the most difficult aspects of the dive to master. It is in this part, however, that most young divers tend to spend the least amount of time working. Study the following information carefully and devote as much time as you can to practice your board work. You can work on it alone, but you will need a coach to assist in the necessary corrections for perfect form.

The Front Approach and Hurdle

The front approach and hurdle is used for all forward-spinning dives and reverse-spinning dives or any forward- or reverse-twisting dives.

1. The Approach The forward approach consists of at least three normal walking steps. According to official rules, you may take more but not less than three steps. Relax and walk normally to the end of the board. Let your arms fall as though they are in a normal walking position. It has been noted that most divers make their final step before the hurdle slightly longer than the others. The last step should end about 18 inches before the end of the board. In this step, allow both arms to swing back in order to be ready to press the board. Finally, allow the knees to bend as you come into the step.

Remember:

a. *Stand at attention at a predetermined place on the board.*

b. *Take at least three relaxed, normal walking steps to a point about 18 inches back from the end of the board.*

c. *Swing both arms back and bend the knee going into the last step.*

2. The Hurdle The hurdle is a skip to the end of the board that comes after the last step. It should be as high as possible and at least 18 inches long and with as much balance as possible.

To begin the hurdle, drive both arms and one leg into the air. (You may use either leg—whichever feels best.) As you leave the board, try to step down with the lead leg by the time you reach the highest point of the hurdle. Just as you drop to the end of the board, swing

both arms backward in a deep circular path. The timing of your arms should be in time with the diving board. New divers tend to encircle their arms too early, causing them to "stomp" the board. Your arms should complete their backward circle just as the board bottoms out.

The ideal hurdle is one that has a very slight forward lean. You will feel as though you are "over" your hurdle rather than being back too far.

Remember:

a. *Drive both arms and one leg up into your hurdle.*

b. *Step down from the top of your hurdle.*

c. *Swing your arms in time with the board.*

d. *Try to feel just slightly over your hurdle.*

The Back Press

The back press sets you up for the takeoff for back or inward-spinning or twisting dives. Here, too, most young divers tend to rush the movements necessary to the back press. Take your time! Enjoy the feeling of being in control.

Begin the back press by standing backward on the end of the board. Your feet should be about halfway over the end and in a comfortable position. Begin the press by slightly dropping your heels to get the board rocking. Then, in time with the board, lift your arms to about a 2 o'clock and 10 o'clock position until you resemble the letter Y. On the downward rock of the board, circle your arms slightly behind you, then deeper, then swing them up in front. During this phase you should be ready to jump.

10 o'clock

Remember:

a. *Stand at the end of the board in a relaxed but at-attention position.*

b. *Start the board gently rocking by dropping your heels.*

c. *In rhythm with the board, lift your arms, then circle to begin your jump.*

16

Lineups and Entries / 4

Before we begin to focus on the movements of the actual dive itself, entries must be studied and practiced first. It takes a long time to develop a good entry into the water, and lots of practice is the only means of achieving it. Start from the side of the pool. Almost anyone can assist by watching you. The following are exercises or drills to pay attention to.

Where to Practice

The best place to learn lineups is from the three-meter board or five-meter platform. Some entry work can be done from the side or from a one-meter board, but you need to get higher to make real progress.

The Grip for a Rip

A rip entry is one that makes very little splash. Its name comes from the fact that if you do it right, it will sound like the ripping of a piece of paper.

Technique:

1. *Place the palm of one hand over the knuckles of the other hand and grab on.*
2. *Keep the palm of your bottom hand facing the water and the hand open.*
3. *As you are about to make contact with the water, "swim" your hands out to your sides as you enter and go underwater. If done right, you will make very little splash. Keep experimenting with your hand position until you find the one that works for you. Have someone watch as you practice.*

Three-Meter Lineups

Practice the following five lineup drills. Work on them at least three days a week.

1. **Forward Lineup: Tuck (Sitting)**
   a. *Sit balanced on the end of the board with your knees drawn up to your chest.*
   b. *Roll forward.*
   c. *Extend out of your tuck position and grasp your hands.*
   d. *Look at the water and line up slightly short.*
   e. *Point your toes!*

2. Forward Lineup: Pike (Sitting)

a. *Sit balanced in a* V *position on the end of the board.*
b. *Hold your arms directly out to your sides.*
c. *Roll forward.*
d. *Extend out of your pike position and grasp your hands.*
e. *Look at the water and line up slightly short.*
f. *Point your toes!*

3. Forward Lineup: Pike (Standing)

Repeat this lineup with the same steps as in No. 2 above but start from a standing position.

4. Back Fall-In Lineup: Layout

a. *Stand backward on the end of the board with your arms out to your sides.*
b. *Fall back toward the water with no arch in your back.*
c. *Just as you leave the board, look back toward the water.*
d. *Line up just short of vertical and grasp your hands.*
e. *Point your toes!*

5. **Back Fall-In: Pike**
   a. *Stand backward on the end of the board and bend forward into a pike position. Hold onto the backs of your calves.*
   b. *Sit toward the water. As you lose your balance and fall, look back and extend from your pike position.*
   c. *Line up just short of vertical and grasp your hands.*
   d. *Point your toes!*

6. **Back Fall-In: Tuck**
   Repeat the fall-in with the same steps as in the pike above but start from a squat position.

Lineups From the Side of the Pool

Lineup drills from the side of the pool are useful for both new and experienced divers. They help you to react quickly to the water and learn how to *save*. They are fun to do, and you can do lots of them in a short time.

1. **Front Lineup: Tuck**
   This is really just a jump to a forward dive tuck. You must be quick to fully extend before you hit the water. Three things to remember are
   a. *Grab before you hit the water.*
   b. *Swim your arms to your sides as you enter the water.*
   c. *Point your toes!*

2. Back Lineup: Layout

To be able to make a back-dive layout, you must jump hard from the side of the pool. Before you hit the water, be sure to

   a. *Look back.*
   b. *Reach back.*
   c. *Grab.*

(*Note:* Be careful not to hit the wall underwater!)

Saves

What Happens Underwater? As you enter the water, you have two choices on where to go. The first is to "take it to the bottom." The second is to "go with the flow." These are called *saves*.

The first save is quite obvious. If you are right where you want to be and can hold your line, go to the bottom of the pool. The second save—go with the flow—means that you continue your spin as you go underwater. For a forward entry, you continue to *roll out* or finish your somersault underwater. With the back entry, you continue to *scoop* underwater and go in that direction.

You will need to concentrate on keeping your knees straight for the forward roll entry and flexing your knees as they go underwater for the back scoop save.

Both of these saves require lots of practice to develop correct timing. You can have someone observe you. With diligent practice, you will develop good lineups, rips, and saves.

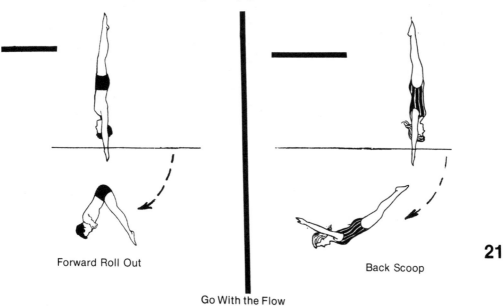

Forward Roll Out

Back Scoop

Go With the Flow

21

A Front Hurdle

The Four Diving Positions / 5

Three body positions are used in the sport of diving. In the numbered list below, four positions are named. They are

1. Layout Position .... Category *A*
2. Pike Position .... Category *B*
3. Tuck Position .... Category *C*
4. Free Position .... Category *D*

The Layout Position

There are two variations of the layout position. One is used for the front, or inward dive. The other is used for back, or reverse-spinning, dive. For the forward dive, you form the letter T with your body. Your arms should be held to the sides with elbows straight and lower back as flat as possible. The back dive is similar except for a slight arch in your back.

Layout Position Drill:

Lie over the edge of a table, arms on the floor, with someone holding your legs. Pull up to the layout position and hold for 30 seconds.

Forward Dive: Pike Position

The Pike Position

The pike position is one of the most attractive positions in diving. It requires a good deal of flexibility. It is useful for some of the spinning dives that you will do as you improve. As you begin using the pike position, keep your head up enough so that you can see over your toes.

Pike Position Drill:

Lie on your back, holding both your legs at the calves just below your knees. Check to be sure that your knees are straight and your toes are pointed.

Keep Your Head Up.

Point Your Toes.

The Tuck Position

The tuck position looks like a diver in a ball position. You bend your body both at the hips and the knees and scrunch up as small as possible. You use the tuck for dives that require multiple rotations (1½ or 2½ somersaults).

You may feel when you are spinning as though you are being pulled out of the tuck. To counteract this feeling, hold onto your shins just below the knees and squeeze. This will help you stay in the position.

24

Keep your head up just enough so that you can see over your knees. The position of your head is important to learn early on. You also must keep your toes pointed while spinning. Learn good habits at the start.

Pike Position

Tuck Position Drills:

1. *From a sitting position with your arms out to the sides, pull your knees into a ball as quickly as possible. Point your toes and grab your shins just below the knees.*

2. *Assume the tuck position while sitting and roll on your back. Try to get as small as possible and squeeze for one minute.*

3. *While in the pool, take a deep breath and get into the tuck position underwater. Squeeze as tight as you can and hold for 30 seconds.*

Tuck Position

The Free Position

The free position is a combination of two or more of the other diving positions used in a preplanned sequence for twisting dives only. The free position is not to be confused with poor execution of other diving positions. Certain dives have requirements for the use of the free position. As you advance, you will learn more about its place in diving.

Reverse Dive - Pike Position

Lead-Ups for the
Basic Dives / 6

Before you learn how to do new dives, you can do *lead-ups*. They are like abbreviated rehearsals that permit you to get the feel of the dives. There are many lead-ups that can help you learn each dive, from the simplest to the more complicated optional ones. If you devote enough time to working on your lead-ups, it will pay off for you later by providing you with the proper *mechanics* of good diving.

Front Dive

The lead-up for the front dive is a simple fall-in. From a standing position on the end of the springboard, bend over, press one leg back, and fall into the water. After you've got the feel of it, remember:

1. *Look at the water.*
2. *Grasp your hands.*
3. *Point your toes.*

As you gain confidence, add a little spring to your dive.

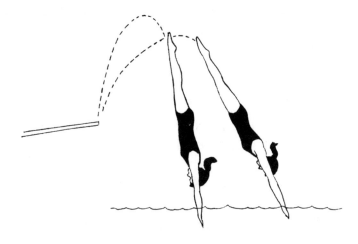

Back Dive

The lead-up for the back dive is a fall-in back dive. Stand backward on the end of the board, with both arms together over your head. Grasp your hands, look back toward the water, and fall! Try not to bend your knees. Don't push. From the one-meter board, you can do a perfect fall-in. As you enter the water, keep your head back and continue the circle underwater.

Reverse Dive

The lead-up for the reverse dive requires you to walk the length of the board. (First measure your steps so that you will be able to land pretty close to the end.) As you reach the end of the board, kick one leg toward the sky and look back toward the board. With determined effort, you'll do a good reverse dive lead-up.

Inward Dive

The best lead-up for the inward dive is an inward dive in the tuck position. Start by standing backward on the end of the board, with your arms over your head. Jump your hips back across the pool and, at the same time, throw both arms down toward the water. On your first try, you probably will enter the water short, but with practice you soon will get better.

The Half Twist

The lead-up for the half twist is much like the front dive: head up, press one leg back, and fall forward. Just as you begin to fall, point one arm and shoulder toward the water, whichever one feels most natural. Before you know it, you will do the half twist.

Now let us get on to the real diving.

Back Dive Layout

The Five Basic
Required Dives / 7

The five basic dives, often referred to as the five required dives, include

1. Front Dive
2. Back Dive
3. Reverse Dive
4. Inward Dive
5. Forward Dive With One-Half Twist

Not all levels of diving demand that these particular dives be done, but they are usually the ones you should learn first. These dives take time to learn. You can be sure that at some time during your career in the sport you will need to use each of these dives.

The Front Dive

The front dive is done from the front hurdle, as described in Chapter 3. The objective of the front dive is to enter the water head first, about four feet in front of the board. The front dive can be done in any of three positions, with the layout being the most common.

The Front Dive: Layout

1. *Reach both arms up after your hurdle. Keep your head up.*

2. *Jump as high as you can. As you begin to leave the board, press both legs behind you. Keep your head up as you jump and look down at the pool.*

3. *Set your arms to the side and keep your back flat. Try to look like the letter* T.

4. *Bring your arms overhead and line up for your entry.*

Front Dive: Layout

The Front Dive: Pike

1. *Reach both arms up after your hurdle. Keep your head up.*

2. *Jump as high as you can and bend over into the pike position as you get to your highest point.*

3. *Keep your eyes on the water and point your toes.*

4. *Press your legs back out of your pike.*

5. *Line up for your entry.*

The Front Dive: Tuck

1. *Reach both arms up after your hurdle. Keep your head up.*

2. *Jump as high as you can and try to get into a tuck position. Keep your eyes on the water.*

3. *Slowly extend from your tuck position and line up for the entry.*

1. THE FRONT DIVE
Layout Position

2. THE BACKWARD DIVE
Layout Position

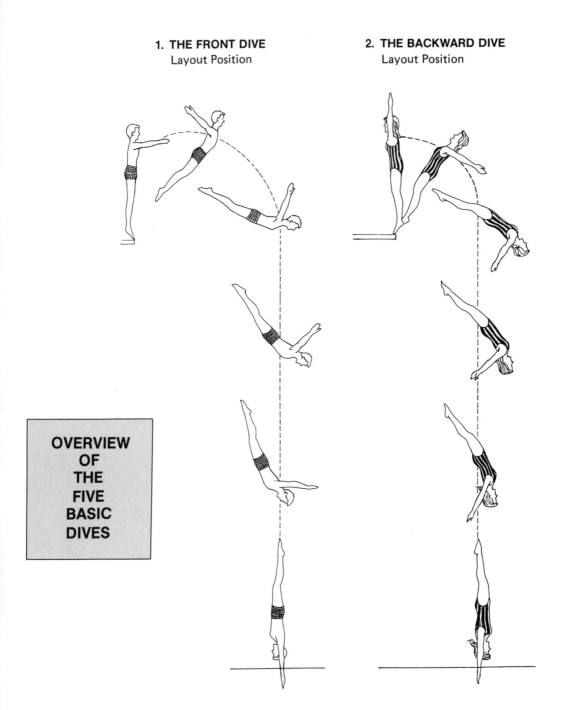

**OVERVIEW
OF
THE
FIVE
BASIC
DIVES**

Competitive Diving is separated in men's and
women's springboard and platform events.

3. THE REVERSE DIVE
Pike Position

4. THE INWARD DIVE
Pike Position

5. THE FORWARD DIVE WITH ONE-HALF TWIST
Layout Position

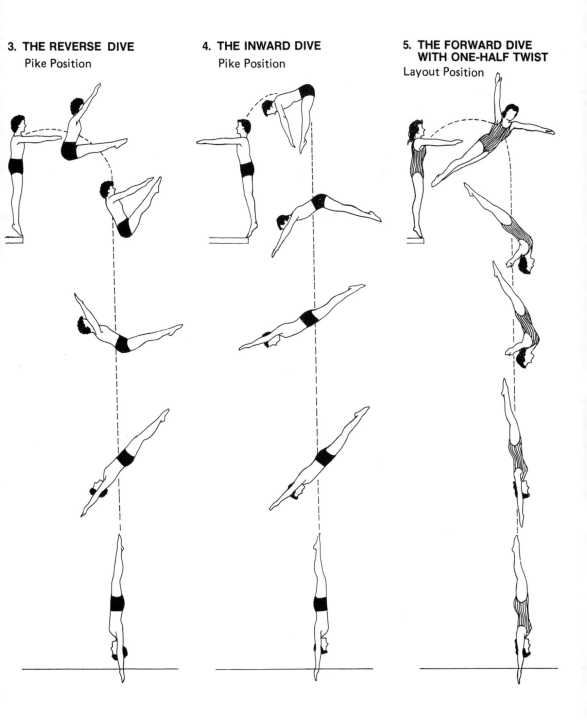

The Back Dive

The back dive is usually done in one of two positions—the layout or pike—with the tuck position seldom used. Practice your back dive in the layout position first, then experiment with the other positions. Begin the back dive by standing backward on the end of the board, using the back press, as described in Chapter 3. The object is to enter the water head first, about three feet from the end of the board and just short of vertical.

The Back Dive: Layout

1. *Jump high into the air, keep your head straight, and reach up over your head.*

2. *As you leave the board, try to get the feel of lifting your chest as you go into the air.*

3. *As your body turns over at the top of your dive, look back toward the water.*

4. *Once you begin to drop toward the water, reach back for your entry.*

The Back Dive: Pike

1. *Jump high into the air, keeping your head straight and arms extended overhead.*

2. *As you rise in the air, bring your legs up to the pike position. Keep looking straight ahead.*

3. *Extend out of your pike and look back toward the water.*

4. *Reach back and line up for your entry.*

The Back Dive: Tuck

1. *Jump high into the air with a very slight backward lean. Keep your head straight by looking at a point directly in front of you. Try to get both arms overhead at the point of the jump.*

Inward Dive: Pike Position

2. *As you leave the board, bring your knees up to the tuck position and keep your head in the same position that it was in when you jumped.*

3. *Kick out of the tuck position by extending at both your hips and knees while looking back toward the water.*

4. *As you assume the extended position, reach back toward the water for your entry.*

The Reverse Dive

The reverse dive, sometimes known as the half gainer, is one of the most spectacular of all dives. It is fun to do and fun to watch. If it is taught and learned properly, it poses no more threat of injury than a front dive. It is simply a good front jump followed by a back dive in the air.

In the beginning, you probably will jump out too far for your reverse dive. With time, practice, and patience, your coordination of the correct movements will land you in just the right spot in the water.

The Reverse Dive: Layout

1. *Jump high into the air, look straight ahead, and reach both arms overhead.*

Back, or Reverse Dive: Layout Position

2. *When you leave the board, lift your chest high into the air as you go toward the highest point of your dive.*

3. *As you begin to drop, look back toward the water.*

4. *Reach back, grasp your hands, and line up for your entry.*

The Reverse Dive: Pike

1. *Jump high into the air, look straight ahead, and reach both arms overhead.*

2. *As you lift into the air, bring both legs up into the pike position. Touch your toes at the highest point of the dive.*

3. *Come out of your pike by pressing away from your legs and looking back toward the water.*

4. *Reach back, grasp your hands, and line up for your entry.*

The Reverse Dive: Tuck

1. *From the front hurdle (learned in Chapter 3) jump high into the air and reach both arms overhead. Try to keep looking straight ahead.*

2. *As you leave the board, bring your legs up to the tuck position. Continue looking straight down at the pool.*

3. *Kick out by extending at the hips and knees at the same time and looking back toward the water.*

4. *Bring your arms together overhead and grasp your hands for your entry.*

The Inward Dive

The inward dive, sometimes called the cutaway or backjack, is a bit scary to most new divers because of the direction of the spin. You must stand backward on the end of the board, jump backward, and spin toward the board. Once you learn it, you will like it because the inward is one of the easiest dives to control.

Whether you choose to master the inward dives in layout, pike, or tuck, you should make it a habit to practice them all. They will prove valuable to you later on as you learn the optional inward dives.

The Inward Dive: Layout

1. *To begin the inward dive start with your back press. Stand backward at the end of the diving board, with your heels extended over the edge. Stand relaxed but in an at-attention position. Start the board gently by dropping your heels and, in rhythm with the board, lift your arms, jump, then circle and bring your arms through while keeping your head up.*

2. *In the jump, drive your legs and hips back and feel yourself slightly over the board with your head and shoulders.*

3. *Assume your layout position as early as possible.*

4. *Grab your hands and line up for your entry.*

(*Note:* The inward dive layout is quite difficult. Let your coach decide when you are ready for it.)

The Inward Dive: Tuck

1. *Again, the inward dive starts with the back press, as described in No. 1 layout above, getting your arms through the circle as you begin your dive.*

2. *As you begin to jump from the board, bring your arms down in front toward the board. At the same time, push your hips up and back.*

3. *Assume your tuck position at the highest point in your dive. Try to keep your eyes on the water throughout your dive.*

4. *Slowly extend out of your tuck position and continue to look at the water. Bring your arms overhead and grasp your hands for your entry.*

Inward Dive: Pike Position

The Inward Dive: Pike

1. *The inward dive starts with the back press and the followup movements as described in No. 1 of the Inward Dive.*

2. *As you jump, try to lift your hips as high as you can. Assume the pike position at the top of your dive.*

3. *Extend out of your dive, continue to look at the water, and grab your hands for your entry.*

The Forward Dive With One-Half Twist

Most divers use the forward dive with one-half twist in the layout position. Thus, we will focus only on that twist in this required dive. Think of this dive in two parts. The first is a one-quarter twist to the highest point of your dive, then a one-quarter twist to the back dive entry.

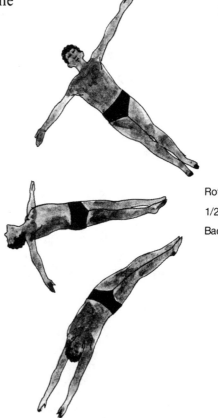

Rotate Your Shoulders
1/2 Twist at Top.
Back Dive Line-Up.

The Forward Dive: One-Half Twist

1. *Use your standard forward approach and hurdle. Try to have both arms overhead at the jump.*

2. *Set your arms in a T position, keep your head up, and slowly rotate your shoulders in the direction that feels best to you —either left or right.*

3. *As you get to the top of your dive, look down at the water and point your lower arm in that same direction.*

4. *Continue to look at the water and line up as if you were doing a back dive.*

You are on your way. These are the five basic dives that you should learn first. As you progress, you will add other dives to your list. When you combine the techniques we have spoken of here with your boardwork, lead-ups, and entries, you will experience the joys of the accomplished diver.

Fundamental Mechanics
of Diving / 8

Fundamental mechanics (or physics) is the subject that deals with the *why* of diving. Why do I go too far? Why don't I go as high as I would like? Why can't I make my somersault? If you can understand the *why* of the problem, it will help you perceive and master particular techniques faster and ease some of the frustrations that you may come up against while you are learning.

Angle of Takeoff

A common problem for beginners is to dive out too far from or too close to the board. The general rule is that the safest distance is about 3 to 4 feet from the end of the board. At that distance, even if you get lost and come out of your dive at the wrong time, you will have no chance of hitting the board. At that distance, you will also have an easier time controlling your rotation.

In order to achieve that distance, you need to lean forward 10° at your *center of gravity*—at the point where you are ready to jump. Your center of gravity is like the middle of a wheel and sits just about in the middle of your body. That is the area you must think about.

Path of Your Center of Gravity

At the very moment you leave the diving board, the path (or flight) of your center of gravity is set. It will follow a curve that is called the *parabolic curve*, and no matter what you do in the air, that path is set. You cannot change direction. If you have too much lean or not enough lean at the point of your jump, you cannot change the path of the curve in the air. So be careful and work diligently for the 10° lean.

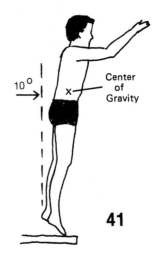

10°

Center
of
Gravity

41

How to Jump Up

In order to jump high, you have to push down. This relates to the great English physicist Isaac Newton's third law of motion: Every action has an equal and opposite reaction. To prove it to yourself, jump up to touch something. Which way do you push the ground?

Stand on the end of the diving board and try the same thing. When you push down, the board moves but you don't go anywhere. Since the board is very flexible and doesn't have a lot of *mass*, it moves quite easily. It will then come back up and try to move *you* into the air. When you dive, you will push the board down from your hurdle. The board is then imbued with *energy*. When the board *bottoms out* (it feels like the floor), you can jump (push against it). The board then returns the energy to you, and you go high into the air. You will need to work on your timing so that you can tell when the board bottoms out so it will help you to jump.

How to Spin

Every dive requires some type of spinning. A simple front dive requires 180° of rotation or a one-half somersault. A forward three-and-one-half somersault requires the same type of spin, only much, much more. You will begin the spin and control the spin in the same way for both dives. Here's how:

1. To get started, push down against the board. Just as you begin to move up, push *forward* to start your body tipping over. If you try this on the ground, you'll start to fall forward. That's rotation. Similarly, if you push backward, you'll spin backward.

2. Get your body moving in the right direction. At the point of takeoff, you'll need to be moving in the direction you want to go. To prove this to yourself, try the game Jump or Dive. If you are going in the wrong direction at the instant you leave the board, you quickly discover that you can't stop in midair in order to go in the correct direction.

3. Be as tall as you can. The more *angular momentum* (intensity of rotational motion) you have, the more somersaults you may be able to do. For the greatest angular momentum, you need to stretch out at the point of takeoff.

Remember:
1. *Push in the opposite direction.*
2. *Move in the direction you want to go.*
3. *Be as tall as you can at the takeoff.*

How to Control Your Spin

Once you are in the air, you can control how fast or slow you spin by getting as small as you can (faster) or as tall as you can (slower). The principles of physics reveal to us that the taller you are, the slower you will spin and the smaller you are, the faster you will spin. Your tuck position enables you to spin faster. Your layout position enables you to spin slower.

How to Stop the Spin

You can't really stop the spin. It is too bad, because that would make diving a lot easier. Physics again reveals that you cannot stop spinning in midair once you have started. (The principle is called *conservation of angular momentum.*) You can slow the spin if you get taller, but you can't stop it.

If you review our discussion on entries, you'll see that you are to grab your hands as you are about to hit the water. This is to help you become as long as possible. You'll slow your spin down perhaps to the point that it seems or looks stopped. Then as you learn to line up a little short and rotate to vertical as you go into the water, your spin may appear to have stopped. But it is all part of the trick that you, the diver, play on those who are watching.

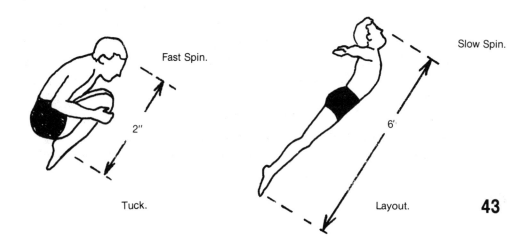

Fast Spin.

2"

Tuck.

Slow Spin.

6'

Layout.

Your Axis of Rotation

When you spin, you spin on an axis that goes from side to side through your middle. When you twist, you twist on an axis that goes from top to bottom. To spin or twist faster, try to get closer to the axis. In other words, get into a tighter tuck.

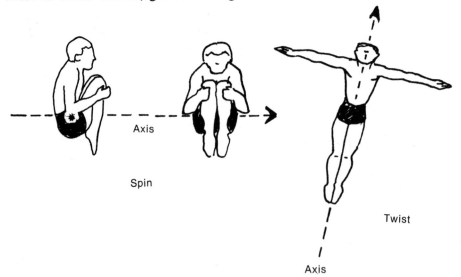

Axis

Spin

Twist

Axis

The Diving Meet / 9

Only when you have attained a certain level in your practice of the basic dives and some optionals will you want to compete. Join a local diving team—either at your school, a Y, Boys' or Girls' Club, or a USA Diving Club. Each group and each meet will have its own requirements for competition. They may include an age limit, degree of difficulty, or number of dives required. Your steps include

1. *Check the requirements.*
2. *Sign up.*
3. *Fill out your diving sheet.*
4. *Meet all the requirements for dives.*
5. *Have fun competing.*

The Day Before

It's not necessary to do every dive perfectly the day before. Many divers leave the dives in practice and have nothing left for the meet. In practice, you want to get used to the pool and board and to get through each of your dives. It is important to the feel of where your dives should be.

There are two things to check before you leave the pool:

1. *What time do you work out and what time is your event scheduled.*
2. *Turn in your diving sheet.*

Pre-Meet Warm-Up

Do your stretch-out exercises early so you'll be ready when the meet starts. You'll probably want to do most of your dives in the warm-up period. Budget your time so that you will make it.

Just Before the Meet

Try to get on the boards again to check your timing and to be sure of the fulcrum settings. This is the time to get your head on straight and to be ready to compete.

During the Meet

There are three guidelines I recommend once the meet starts:
1. *Concentrate.* This will help you do your best dives during the meet.
2. *Do your best.* Don't save anything. Go for every dive the best way you know how.
3. *Have fun.* Every sport is aimed at having fun. Be a good winner. Be a good loser. This is your opportunity to show what you can do, to have fun, and to make friends. Make the most of it.

Scoring the Diving Meet

The diver who wins the diving meet is the one who scores the most points. Each dive is rated by the three judges on a scale from 0 to 10 at ½-point intervals. The better the dive, the better the score. The total from the judges is then added together and multiplied by a number called the *degree of difficulty.* It's a rating scale that goes from 1.2 to 3.5 and represents how hard the dive is to perform. This score is added up for each dive that you do. *Example:*

Judges score	5
	4½
	6½'
Judges total	16
Degree of difficulty ×	2.2
Dive total award	35.2

The number of dives that you do and the number of categories that you must cover will depend on your age, the type of meet, and the level of competition (local, county, state, or national).

Afterword

No one really knows what the future holds for the sport of competitive diving. Nor does anyone know what the sport will demand of its divers. Not that many years ago, it was commonly thought that a forward two-and-one-half somersault in the pike position from the one-meter board was impossible. Now, not only do most men and many women collegiate divers use it in their repertoire of dives, many divers in younger age groups use it without a second thought.

There is really no limit for the divers of the United States, or even a limit to the difficulty of some of the dives that are done. We easily can imagine forward four-and-one-half or five-and-one-half somersaults or quadruple or quintuple twisting optional dives. Some of you reading this book may eventually be working on those dives. You will do them and you will do them beautifully.

Those of you who will enter the sport in the future will be better trained and better managed competitors than we have ever had before. Your opportunities have never been greater. So, go for it! Get out there, train hard, have fun, and make wonderful friendships.

B.G.

INDEX